People and Possessions

30 unique postcards

© 2002 New Internationalist Publications Ltd, Oxford
and individual photographers
www.newint.org

Design by Andrew Kokotka
British Library Cataloguing-in-Publication Data.
A catalogue record for this book is available from the British Library.

ISBN   0 9540499 4 2

Printed by C & C Offset Printing Co. Ltd., Hong Kong.

From the book
Material World, Sierra Club Books (1994)
And other photographs by Peter Menzel et al.

PEOPLE & POSSESSIONS

Welcome to *People & Possessions*. In a ground-breaking innovative project, 16 of the world's foremost photographers, led by Peter Menzel, travelled to 30 nations across the globe to live for a week with 'average' families in each of them. At the end of their stay a portrait was taken of the family outside their home, surrounded by all their belongings – a few jugs and a bed for some, an explosion of electronic gadgetry for others.

These postcards are the collection of such global family portraits, organised alphabetically, from Albania to Western Samoa. Taken between 1993 and 2001, they include two pictures of the Demirovic-Bucalovic family from Sarejevo, Bosnia. The first was taken when the city had been under siege by Serb militia for twenty months. If you look carefully you can see not just the United Nations soldiers but also where the apartment balcony has been hit by an incoming shell. The second was taken in 2001 after the fighting had stopped, the building had been repaired and UN troops had departed.

Taken together the collection of pictures vividly portrays the look and feel of the human condition across the world. It highlights what we share, as well as our differences. Not least, it contrasts the material wealth of some with the deprivation of others.

Ask yourself what would happen to humanity if everyone possessed as much, or lived in the same way as the average family in Japan or the United States. It's not just that some have too much and others too little. The real value of things depends on their use, and the environment in which they are located.

Go ahead and discover how the photos speak for themselves – the detail in the landscapes, the houses, the size of the family, their religion and dress. Not least check out the facial expressions and what they might be telling us.

Whilst you are thinking about it, why not send someone a family portrait postcard?

CONTENTS

► NEW INTERNATIONALIST PUBLICATIONS ► WWW.NEWINT.ORG

► THE CAKONI FAMILY ► ALBANIA ► PHOTO: LOUIS PSIHOYOS & JOHN KNOEBBER

► NEW INTERNATIONALIST PUBLICATIONS ► WWW.NEWINT.ORG
► THE CARBALLO FAMILY ► ARGENTINA ► PHOTO: PETER GINTER

► NEW INTERNATIONALIST PUBLICATIONS ► WWW.NEWINT.ORG
► THE NAMGAY FAMILY ► BHUTAN ► PHOTO: PETER MENZEL

► NEW INTERNATIONALIST PUBLICATIONS ► WWW.NEWINT.ORG

► THE DEMIROVIC-BUCALOVIC FAMILY ► BOSNIA 1993 ► PHOTO: ALEXANDRA BOULAT

► NEW INTERNATIONALIST PUBLICATIONS ► WWW.NEWINT.ORG

► THE DEMIROVIC-BUCALOVIC FAMILY ► BOSNIA 2001 ► PHOTO: PETER MENZEL

▶ NEW INTERNATIONALIST PUBLICATIONS ▶ WWW.NEWINT.ORG
▶ THE DE GOES FAMILY ▶ BRAZIL ▶ PHOTO: PETER GINTER

▶ NEW INTERNATIONALIST PUBLICATIONS ▶ WWW.NEWINT.ORG
▶ THE WU FAMILY ▶ CHINA ▶ PHOTO: LEONG KA TAI

► NEW INTERNATIONALIST PUBLICATIONS ► WWW.NEWINT.ORG
► THE COSTA FAMILY ► CUBA ► PHOTO: PETER MENZEL

▶ NEW INTERNATIONALIST PUBLICATIONS ▶ WWW.NEWINT.ORG
▶ THE PFITZNER FAMILY ▶ GERMANY ▶ PHOTO: PETER GINTER

► NEW INTERNATIONALIST PUBLICATIONS ► WWW.NEWINT.ORG

► THE CALABAY SICAY FAMILY ► GUATEMALA ► PHOTO: MIGUEL LUIS FAIRBANKS

► NEW INTERNATIONALIST PUBLICATIONS ► WWW.NEWINT.ORG
► THE YADAV FAMILY ► INDIA ► PHOTO: PETER GINTER

► NEW INTERNATIONALIST PUBLICATIONS ► WWW.NEWINT.ORG
► THE ZAKS FAMILY ► ISRAEL ► PHOTO: PETER GINTER

► NEW INTERNATIONALIST PUBLICATIONS ► WWW.NEWINT.ORG
► THE PELLEGRINI FAMILY ► ITALY ► PHOTO: PETER GINTER

▶ NEW INTERNATIONALIST PUBLICATIONS ▶ WWW.NEWINT.ORG
▶ THE UKITA FAMILY ▶ JAPAN ▶ PHOTO: PETER MENZEL

▶ NEW INTERNATIONALIST PUBLICATIONS ▶ WWW.NEWINT.ORG
▶ THE ABDULLA FAMILY ▶ KUWAIT ▶ PHOTO: PETER MENZEL

► NEW INTERNATIONALIST PUBLICATIONS ► WWW.NEWINT.ORG
► THE NATOMO FAMILY ► MALI ► PHOTO: PETER MENZEL

► NEW INTERNATIONALIST PUBLICATIONS ► WWW.NEWINT.ORG

► THE CASTILLO BALDERAS FAMILY ► MEXICO ► PHOTO: PETER MENZEL

▶ NEW INTERNATIONALIST PUBLICATIONS ▶ WWW.NEWINT.ORG
▶ THE REGZEN FAMILY ▶ MONGOLIA ▶ PHOTO: LEONG KA TAI & PETER MENZEL

► NEW INTERNATIONALIST PUBLICATIONS ► WWW.NEWINT.ORG
► THE KAPRALOV FAMILY ► RUSSIA ► PHOTO: LOUIS PSIHOYOS & JOHN KNOEBBER

▶ NEW INTERNATIONALIST PUBLICATIONS ▶ WWW.NEWINT.ORG
▶ THE DE FRUTOS FAMILY ▶ SPAIN ▶ PHOTO: JOSE MÁNUEL NAVIA

▶ NEW INTERNATIONALIST PUBLICATIONS ▶ WWW.NEWINT.ORG
▶ THE KUANKAEW FAMILY ▶ THAILAND ▶ PHOTO: PETER MENZEL

► NEW INTERNATIONALIST PUBLICATIONS ► WWW.NEWINT.ORG
► THE ÇINAR FAMILY ► TURKEY ► PHOTO: PETER MENZEL

► NEW INTERNATIONALIST PUBLICATIONS ► WWW.NEWINT.ORG
► THE CAVIN FAMILY ► UNITED STATES ► PHOTO: PETER MENZEL

▶ NEW INTERNATIONALIST PUBLICATIONS ▶ WWW.NEWINT.ORG

▶ THE KALNAZAROV FAMILY ▶ UZBEKISTAN ▶ PHOTO: LOUIS PSIHOYOS & JOHN KNOEBBER

► NEW INTERNATIONALIST PUBLICATIONS ► WWW.NEWINT.ORG
► THE NGUYEN FAMILY ► VIETNAM ► PHOTO: LEONG KA TAI

► NEW INTERNATIONALIST PUBLICATIONS ► WWW.NEWINT.ORG

► THE LAGAVALE FAMILY ► WESTERN SAMOA ► PHOTO: PETER MENZEL

ABOUT PETER MENZEL

Peter Menzel is a California-based photojournalist whose work has appeared in many national and international magazines including *National Geographic, Time, Newsweek, Discover, Smithsonian, Wired, Geo,* and *Stern.*

Menzel's projects have included the books *Material World, A Global Family Portrait* (1994), *Women in the Material World* (co-authored with his wife, Faith D'Aluisio) (1996), and *Man Eating Bugs: the Art and Science of Eating Insects*, (co-authored with Faith D'Aluisio (1998). Menzel and his wife recently completed their fourth photographic book, *Robo sapiens: Evolution of a New Species* (2000). Menzel's initial robot photo-reportage for Stern Magazine that led to the book *Robo sapiens* was awarded first place for science photography by World Press Photo 2000 in Amsterdam.

Peter Menzel lives in Napa, California, with his wife, Faith D'Aluisio. They have four teenage sons.

Vanishing Footprints – Nomadic People Speak

by Anthony Swift & Ann Perry

This book captures something of the variety of nomadic cultures, from the savannahs of Africa or the rain forests of the Amazon basin to the snowbound areas within the Arctic Circle. Over 120 colour photos give stunning insights and illuminate the main themes.

The World Guide 2001/2002

An alternative reference to the countries of our planet.

Researched and written in the South, this essential reference work is an invaluable key to understanding global issues, as well as a definitive guide to the countries of the world. It provides a wealth of information unavailable elsewhere.

Festive Foods: Christmas Dishes from Around the World

by Hanne Kruse

The idea of a Christmas feast has spread throughout the world, where food and traditions surrounding the Festive Season have been coloured by local habits and cuisine. For many, the Christmas meal is the most important dinner of the year. This book will provide plenty of inspiration. Foreword by Archbishop Desmond Tutu.

The New Internationalist Magazine

See the world through fresh eyes – read the *New Internationalist* monthly magazine. It is the only magazine of its kind offering an insight into the important issues that face our world. Each issue tackles one subject in depth. It could be Human

Rights or Globalisation, Aid or the Arms Trade. The ideas, the facts and arguments are all carefully edited with clear charts, lively articles, superb colour photos and vivid graphics to give you the whole picture. Contact the New Internationalist for a free copy.

A full catalogue of all New Internationalist publications is available from your nearest New Internationalist office (addresses below) or visit our web site:

www.newint.org

UNITED KINGDOM & EUROPE
55 Rectory Road
Oxford OX4 1BW
Tel: +44 1865 811400
E-mail: ni@newint.org

IRISH REPUBLIC
PO Box 8115
Dublin 15
Tel: +353 1 811 5970
E-mail: ni@dna.ie

CANADA/US
1011 Bloor Street West
Toronto
Ontario M6H 1M1
E-mail: nican@web.ca

AUSTRALIA AND PNG
28 Austin Street
Adelaide
SA 5000
Tel: +61 8 8232 1563
E-mail:
sandyl@newint.com.au

AOTEAROA/NEW ZEALAND
PO Box 4499
Christchurch
Tel: +64 3 3656 153
E-mail:
newint@chch.planet.org.nz

REST OF WORLD
Please contact the UK office